FROM

Sherry,
Thank you
your support.
Be Blessed :)
Dr. Regn Spellm

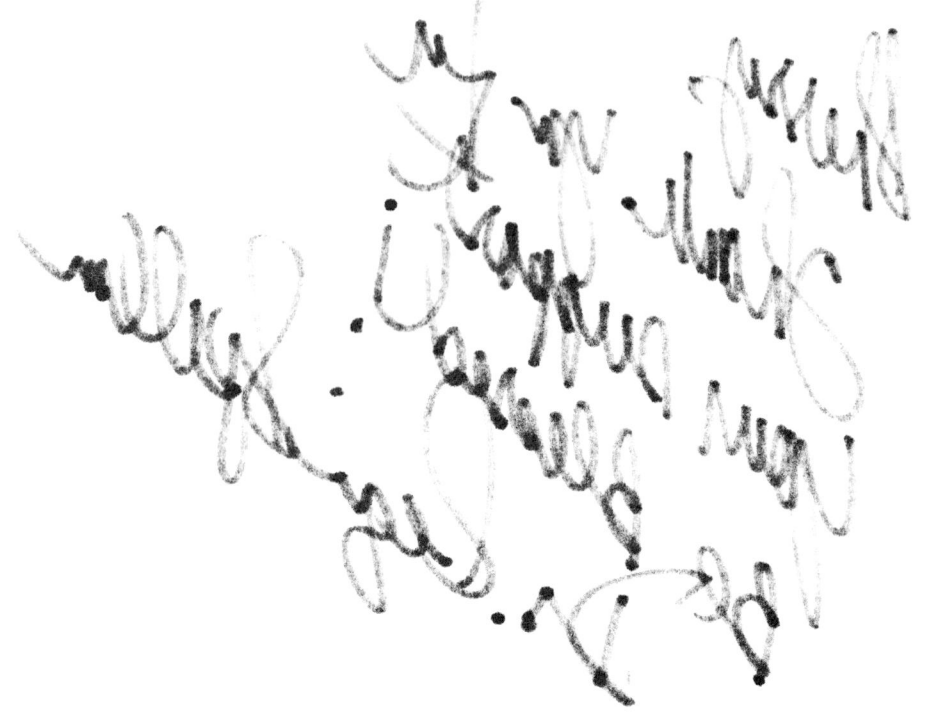

FROM PIECES TO PEACE

FROM PIECES TO PEACE

Dr. Regina Spellmon

Unless otherwise indicated all scriptural quotations are taken from the King James Version of the Bible.

FROM PIECES TO PEACE
Copyright © 2015
Dr. Regina Spellmon
Regina Spellmon Ministries

Printed in the United States of America

Library of Congress – Catalogued in Publication Data

ISBN 978-0692386255

<u>Published by:</u>
Jabez Books Writers' Agency
(A Division of Clark's Consultant Group)
www.clarksconsultantgroup.com

All rights reserved. No part of this book may be reproduced, stored in a retrieval system, or transmitted in any form or by any means, electronic, mechanical photocopying, recording, or otherwise, without written consent of the publisher except in the case of brief quotations in critical articles or reviews.

Endorsements

Is it possible to go from hurt to wholeness? Regardless of where you are in your *production* called life, *From Pieces to Peace*, tells you the answer is a resounding Yes! This book assures and encourages you that God is *for* you and *with* you every step of the way. Dr. Regina Spellmon has done a masterful job of showing us how to reach our God-given destiny despite experiencing disruptions along the way. A must read.

> Kevin K. Dickerson, Senior Pastor
> Dayspring Family Church
> Irving, TX

Dr. Regina has captured something very special here. She is living proof of the grace and mercy of our Savior. Jesus never promised us that following Him would not bring pain and suffering. He did promise us His peace. Dr. Regina leaves no stone unturned in this very revealing and inspiring book. A must read.

> Pastors Norris and Tonya McGill
> Founding Pastors
> Antioch Christian Church
> Irving, TX

My wife and I have had the tremendous opportunity to have Dr. Spellmon minister to the women of His Tabernacle Family Church multiple years in a row. She not only loves and serves Jesus, but loves and cares for His people. She ministered the Word with power and the anointing, which has released and healed the hearts of many women of the church and community.

We were also privileged to be present at her ordination, and to preach from her pulpit. She is a woman of character, which was proven through difficulties that she experienced in her life. When the dust cleared, she was still standing! We are blessed to know Dr. Spellmon and to have her in our lives not only in ministry, but in our heart. Dr. Spellmon is without question a genuine, authentic woman of God!

> Dr. Micheal & Rhonda Spencer
> His Tabernacle Family Church
> Horseheads, New York

"From Pieces to Peace" is real, raw, and powerful. And it was written by a woman who has known the depths of despair, and was able to overcome with grace and dignity.

> Sue Detweiler
> Author, Speaker & Pastor

With courage, clarity, confidence, and compassion, Dr. Regina Spellmon shares her story. Her authenticity is heart-warming and her sacrifice is obvious; both will be a blessing to many. You won't be able to put this book down!

Pastor Sonjia Dickerson, Co-Pastor
Dayspring Family Church
Irving, TX

Dr. Spellmon is a dynamic proclaimer of the gospel who uses creativity and transparency to engage with her audiences. Through real-life experiences, she shares her most fractured parts to offer pieces of wholeness to those who read her story. Her resilience and undying faith gives readers strength to endure the struggle, and hope to persevere through all of life's challenges!

Pastor and Lady J
Higher Dimension Church
Houston, TX

Thank You

- Mom and Dad (Willie Hathman)

You are by far the strongest people I know. Your sacrifices have been limitless. You have created a life for me beyond my level of understanding. Although life seemed to have brought many heartaches in our lives, but I now realized; we were built for it from the beginning. Your strength, stamina, and commitment have been an example for me and many others. I can't thank you enough for the woman I have become. Thank you for believing in me and encouraging me along my journey. You gave me life and then encouraged me to live it abundantly. I love you both.

- Ambassadors Today

Thank you family for giving me life when I literally thought I was going to die. You have caused me to live again. Thanks for believing in me. Thanks for trusting me. Thanks for encouraging me, and most of all, thank you for allowing God to use the broken pieces of my life, so that the Excellency of His power could shine through. I am blessed and forever grateful to be your Pastor. I love you all.

- Support Team of Ladies

A special thanks to the ladies that sat up with me at nights on end, typing, writing, and listening to complete this chapter in my life. I thank God for you!

Table of Contents

Prologue 17

Let the Show Begin! 29

Act I Scene I: My Early Years 39

Act I Scene II: My Adolescent Years 65

INTERMISSION

Act I Scene III: My High School Years 91
Revisit the Script

INTERMISSION

Now, On With the Production 108

Act II Scene I: Getting It Together   115

Act II Scene II: Delivered, But Not Free   131

Act II Scene III: This is Not What I Had   147
                             In Mind

Prologue

As I sip from my favorite cup of coffee, sitting outside on the balcony, in my old faithful comfortable chair, peace and gratitude overtake me as I enjoy the skyline and the warm breeze gingerly caressing my face. You see, it hasn't always been like this, and it had been a long time since I was able to sit and enjoy the simple things in life. I haven't always been comfortable in my own skin, let alone in a beautiful setting like I'm in right now.

And as my mind wanders back to a time, just a few years ago, I could be found in the corner of a small room, a rental home that was poorly lit. There was no hot water and none of the comforts of home. It was the parallel opposite of how I had been living up to that point in my life. I was living at the opposite end of the spectrum, so to speak. Sometimes I wasn't sure if I wanted to keep breathing, because I was so wounded that each breath felt like a knife was being driven deeper into my soul.

Part of what made it even worse was that I couldn't just curl up and die, instead I had to be strong. Regardless of how I felt, I still knew I had a calling on my life that needed to be lived out. God wasn't finished working through me. There were people depending on me; so no matter how much it hurt I had to continue on.

My pain didn't start at the part of the story people think they know; instead my pain started as pieces began to be ripped from me early in my life. Piece by piece, my spirit was being torn apart from almost the very beginning. Piece by piece, my will was being tested as my life felt like it was being shattered.

One thing I have learned, based on my life, is that destiny always comes with disruptions. Each distraction and dart that is aimed towards you will be followed by deliverance. What is intended to be a weapon used to take you out is actually used as a step to take you higher in Him.

For every tear I cried, a tiny flame was lit within me. If it weren't for God keeping me safe from my own inner flames, as well as the fiery darts being thrown at me from my onlookers, I would have been burned beyond ashes long ago.

Instead God's Word describes it best when it says, "He'll give us beauty for ashes." Has life burned you time and time again? Don't worry; God also uses fire to remove our impurities. I found that sometimes firemen have to start a fire to put out a fire.

When a goldsmith refines gold, he uses fire hotter than any other source of heat it has ever been exposed to in order to change the gold from its original state of being. The gold being at first mixed with things that add no value is reduced to its most vulnerable state. The fire is so hot that it changes what at first was hard as rock into a liquid pliable state. This vulnerability is necessary to complete the purification process.

The purer the gold, the more beautiful it becomes, which causes it to increase in value. We, of course, are already invaluable. And the experience of going through the fire increases our value as well. When we survive a flame hotter and more intense than the last, we are able to share our story with an even greater passion with others who need to know it. People who are feeling the effects of their own purification processes are wondering if they will make it through.

Without our stories to encourage them, their focus is easily and understandably on the flame itself, instead of the benefits of the process.

When we are able to let others hear that we have been as vulnerable and uncomfortable as they are now, a glimmer of hope can be formed. Also, as we agree and are able to acknowledge that their experiences do legitimately hurt, we are able to let them know there is a *Comforter* that makes the difference. Therefore we are able to let others know that with God ALL things *truly* are possible and their situation is not bigger than the Word of God.

> *When we do not dwell on the circumstances we are going through, no matter how traumatic or horrific they are, but instead focus on the One who will deliver us, we show God that we do trust Him.*

Beauty for ashes doesn't mean we will never be burned. Nor does it mean we will never be in the fire again. What it does mean is that even in the hardest, hottest times, God is still with us and in control. God is able to take our "horrors" to create hope for ourselves as well as those needing to hear our stories. God uses our worst pains to show us that what we thought would kill us, will not, because He is there. It may sound horrible, but without the experiences we have faced, we would have never known God in that way, nor would we have seen or known for ourselves the truth that with God there are no limits.

I am by no means someone who enjoys pain and discomfort, but knowing now that if my wounds can touch and heal another person, I am able to better appreciate each and every tear I shed. I would willingly endure it all over again if I knew it would make a difference in your life.

Isaiah 26:3 says, "We will have perfect peace if we keep our mind stayed on Him."

This shows a sign of trust. When we do not dwell on the circumstances we are going through, no matter how traumatic or horrific they are, but instead focus on the One who will deliver us, we show God that we do trust Him. And neither height nor depth, nor rape or drugs, nor alcohol nor any other form of abuse can separate us from the love of God. It also shows Him that we know that truly with Him all things are possible.

Perfect peace, when we are perfectly in pieces, is obtainable when we focus on the solution not the problem. I have often said that the more broken we are, the more we can help others piece by piece. This is still true. I have been torn, crushed, shattered and broken into more and more pieces, but I never lost a single bit of value. You see, finding peace no matter what state I am in makes the difference. No, it does not mean; I will never cry. No, it does not mean, it does not hurt. Yes, it might hurt and I might even cry, but there is still hope because I know where my help comes from.

My help comes from the Lord, the true Author and Finisher of my faith. Because He has this role in my story, I have confidence that with God in my life, the story is only finished when He says so. Because of this hope, no matter what state I am in, He can restore me.

Pieces to Peace, is a tour of some of my most broken times in my life. But the most wonderful thing is that the tour does not end piece by piece, but instead it continues on peace by peace.

Let the Show Begin!

"Ladies and gentlemen, welcome to the show tonight! We are so glad you joined us. Hi, my name is Dr. Regina Spellmon and I will be your narrator tonight. I'm absolutely ecstatic that you have chosen to go with me on a journey of a lifetime. Together, we are about to embark upon an intriguing story of someone's life who has endured insurmountable challenges. However, by the grace of God, she made it through. It is what we call a testimony."

****

I have often thought of our lives as a "Production," a screen written play where God is the Producer. It has a script with very detailed-oriented information that causes us to learn from each scene. Scenes where God uses characters with different roles, like you and I, so that each person can play out their role to achieve the result He intended for our lives.

So what you are about to experience is a depiction of what many of you would call "drama-filled" scenes. At times, you will encounter joy and laughter. At other times, tears, horror, anger, frustration, and intense emotions might occur as you travel through the sequences of this story.

I'm aware of the fact that this production has not come to its conclusion; yet, by the simple fact that the main character of this story is still alive. Also, I am positive of the fact that God is steadily adding lines and switching characters to assure that the main character reaches her destiny. Nevertheless, the scenes that have been played out, I believe, should receive standing ovations, because of its anticipated impact in delivering many who will read it.

Now let's go over the house rules:

- You must have an open heart and mind as the acts are played out.

- Get a box of tissues, so that you can have them on hand if you need them.

- Be prepared to apply any lesson that you may learn from each scene, keeping in mind, we are all characters in this journey called life.

- If you are like the masses, many of them have to practice, practice, and practice to maintain the leading role.

And as Christians, they have to continue to support and communicate with the other actors and actresses who are also placed in the production with them (the Holy Spirit, family, friends, etc.), so that they can constantly assess their position. With all of their joined efforts, this will turn out exactly how the Producer wanted. It may not be the way the actors/actresses think it should have been played out, but they are not the Producer. So without any further ado, let's dim the lights and set the stage for God's production in the life of an incredible woman – Dr. Regina Spellmon.

In The Beginning

Every production has a beginning!

Just like when God created Adam and Eve in

the Garden of Eden in the book of Genesis. The Bible records it this way:

"In the beginning God created the heavens and the earth. Now the earth was formless and empty, darkness was over the surface of the deep, and the Spirit of God was hovering over the waters. And God said, "Let there be light, and there was light." (Genesis 1:1-2)

My "genesis" started on October 18, 1960

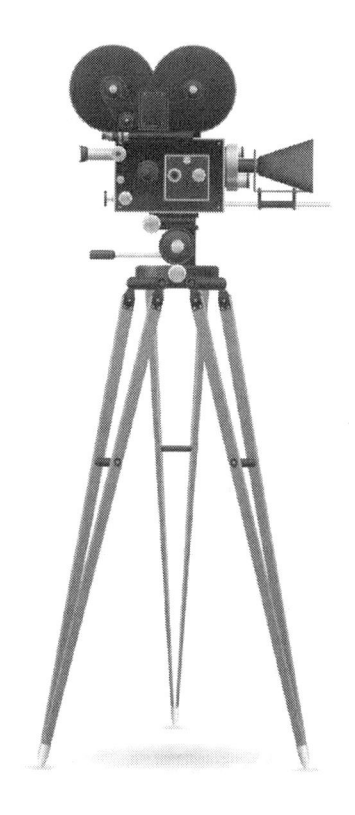

Act I, Scene I: Early Years

Setting: Fall of 1960, Chicago, Illinois

Characters: Regina, Her Mother, and a Few Extras

When I was born, October 18, 1960, in Chicago, Illinois, my mother gave birth to me on a fragile kitchen table in a small-thin walled efficiency apartment that housed three people. Back then, these types of apartments were called flats, and we were fortunate enough to have a three-room unit.

When my mother started having contractions, she could sense it was time for her to give birth, so she told her husband to call her sister, Grace, and the doctor. The first one on the scene was her sister, who was only 15 to 20 minutes away. Then shortly after this, the nurse arrived. They washed up and put a sheet on the dining room table to cover it. Then she was told to lie on the table. She said it was an easy delivery, so much so that she wanted six more children UNTIL she had my brother.

Once I was born, the nurse stayed a little while to make sure everything was okay, and then she left. But she thanked God for her sister for caring for her after the medical team left. When I think back on how I was born on a kitchen table, I know I was destined to be unique from the start.

Maybe you were born in a unique situation or conceived in a way that may taunt you today, but I'm here to tell you that no matter how you arrived, God has you HERE on earth for a purpose.

Many of my earlier years are a blur, but I do remember growing up with my mom as she tried to work and make ends meet constantly. Being young and clueless, I assumed she was both my mother and father, because I never saw a male figure that played that role for a significant period in my life. It was always my mom and I and this was enough for me.

Obviously my mother was in a relationship that I wasn't aware of, because supposedly after a major altercation with her male companion, the two of us found ourselves switching from a three room to a two room flat with a bedroom and a kitchen. We stayed there as long as we could afford. Then we found ourselves on a train ride headed to Palestine, TX. It was the nearest train stop to Tennessee Colony. I was only two years old, but I remember being excited about being on a bumpy train for hours.

When we arrived in Palestine, TX, we stayed with my grandmother. However, as soon as my mother could start looking for a job, she did. Now, it was the sixties, employment and steady jobs were very difficult for Black Americans to get, especially if you were a female. My mom tried with much determination to land a job that would support her and this addition that had intruded her life unexpectedly—me.

You see, before my mother was pregnant with me, she was attending college in Chicago hoping to become an accountant. She borrowed money to fulfill the dream in her heart, but pregnancy precluded this dream. Regardless, my mother was a real powerhouse. Even though it was a struggle for her to find employment, she persevered no matter what and became the first black female to obtain a job at "Buddies Supermarket Delicatessen," in Fort Worth, TX, which was later known as Winn Dixie. In that era, the income she earned was enough to make ends meet and to keep a decent roof over our heads. Yet, it was not without sacrifices.

I recall every day after school juggling from being a student, to trying to retain knowledge, to this inexperience "adult" trying to prepare TV dinners for dinner and preparing myself for the next day's duties. Perhaps, this is why I don't care for TV dinner type foods today. It reminds me of these times in my life. It is amazing how we respond to things as adults because of what we experienced as a child.

I would sit at home alone many days, and as an adolescent, I was expected to do the right thing, but I am sure you know I did not do the right thing all the time. Some days I was successful, some days I was not. Every now and then I would try to cook against my mother's wishes. That ended quickly after my dress caught on fire trying to fry livers. God covers fools and babies, *laughing out loud*. But for the most part, I was a good kid, and I did do what was expected of me.

However, I cannot say this was true when I was in grade school. In those days, I was attending a private Catholic school. Yes; you guessed it. I stayed in the "confession booth" all the time. It seemed like I was always doing something that kept me "confessing my sins." And I especially hated *Ash Wednesday*, because I did not like having ashes on my forehead! I would always wash it off as soon as I could. So when my

> *During those years, I did not see my mother much. I have to honestly say there were many times I wondered if my mother really loved me, because I never spent time with her.*

mother allowed me to attend public school, I was thrilled. I am not sure why she moved me, but it meant no more Ash Wednesday's.

During those years, I did not see my mother much. I have to honestly say there were many times I wondered if my mother really loved me, because I never spent time with her. I would see her in passing type situations, meaning she was headed in while I was heading out. This went on for a few years until I was old enough to start inquiring about the male figure in her life.

Somewhere in the first couple of years of my mother being in Texas, she met a man. At first, he would come over to the house sporadically. Then he started coming around a lot more than usual, which elicited questions in my mind about my father. I used to wonder:

- Who birthed me?
- Whose name was in the father's section on my birth certificate?
- Who was it that was not able to attend the father and daughter activities at my school?
- Who was this person?

I never knew who my father was. Nor did I think much about it until I was in middle school. I do specifically recall when we had father and daughter activities at my school that I would begin to think about it and question it internally. Of course, I never voiced it to my mother, so I would dismiss it from my mind as soon as the activities had passed.

Then one day, finally, I discovered my father's name. I was overwhelmed with joy. I finally knew who my father was; at least that's what I thought. I saw my birth certificate for the first time, and the name that was written for my father, was Roosevelt. I didn't remember him, but I felt somewhat slightly consoled that I had a name. Only to find out many years later, he was not actually my biological father.

You see, when my mother got pregnant with me, while attending college, she really wanted to do the right thing. She knew it would break her father's heart knowing she was pregnant and not married. So she was blessed to meet a wonderful man that loved her and accepted her regardless of the fact that she was pregnant with another man's child. He cared so deeply for her, and she cared for him. They talked about her situation and agreed to get married. His name was Roosevelt. They were only married for two years. However, my mother will be forever grateful to him because he was there when she really needed a friend and a confidant. Even though she had to drop out of college; he made her situation so much better by loving her and supporting her throughout her ordeal.

And the only other man I ever knew was my mom's new boyfriend. A six foot tall, light skinned guy she met while working at the United States Post Office. She had gotten a job as a clerk at the Post Office where he was a mail clerk at the time. He had been married before and had six girls. I think that is what attracted both of us to him. I recall one day my mom was so impressed, because he had decided to take me to a movie, and when she came home, he had combed my hair as well. We knew then; he was a real keeper. Obviously he was, because they married, and have been married 47 years.

One summer, like my mother had done in years past, I was sent to live with my grandmother. But when I returned home one particular summer, I was greeted by a pregnant mother. She was pregnant with my nine years younger sibling, Eric. It was not something I was excited about. I had been the only child for a long time, and it felt weird to have a younger brother that I had to look after when he was born. I remember times that I would deliberately try to harm him just to make him go away.

One day, I was in the kitchen and Eric was in a car seat on the table. I noticed that when I would make him laugh, the car seat would move closer to the edge of the table. Now, what would a big sister who's tired of her younger brother do? I continued to make him laugh until the car seat hit the kitchen floor, face down. I ran as fast as I could so I wouldn't be around to get blamed for the incident, but it didn't work. I paid for that one! I know this story was not the greatest moment in my life, but it is amazing what a child will do when they feel their place in a family is being threatened. And thank God, my brother was not seriously injured, and like I said, I paid dearly for this one.

A lot of times things happen in our lives that we may not want or approve, however, we must realize all of it has purpose, meaning and value, regardless of how we feel about it. Those very things, no

> *A lot of times things happen in our lives that we may not want or approve of, however, we must realize all of it has purpose, meaning and value, regardless of how we feel about it.*

matter how much resistance we had to them at first, will be turned around and work for our good. Even though I definitely did not want to be a big sister, at first, I cannot imagine living my life now without my younger brother.

Eventually, I got over the shock of having a brother, and I realize now a lot of my behavior or response toward him stemmed from the fact that I rarely spent time with my mother before he came on the scene. I knew he would take up some of the time I wanted, and so desperately needed to spend with my mother.

> *There was nothing in the physical that told me that Roosevelt was not my biological father, but there was an innate yearning for something I had no knowledge of.*

As time passed, I did adjust accordingly, but from time to time, there would be a strange feeling inside of me longing for a man I never knew — my biological father. There was nothing in the physical that told me that Roosevelt was not my biological father, but there was an innate yearning for something I had no knowledge of. From time to time I would say something to my mother about this, so eventually in my early teenage years, my mother sat me down and told me the man that I thought was my father was not really my father.

The truth was finally revealed. There was a man who lived in Chicago, who was actually my biological dad. I could not believe what I was hearing. But it made sense when I thought about this undeniable desire to meet someone I never knew existed.

That's when my search and quest for him began.

I wanted to not only know him; I wanted him to be a part of my life. So I made every opportunity to make contact with him, and thanks to my mother's sister, who assisted me in my quest, I was able to locate him.

My mother's sister lived in Chicago and she was familiar with my father. She researched and found his phone number and address. After two to three months, I was able to connect with my biological father for the first time in my life. Thanks to my aunt and my mom, I talked to my dad on the phone for the first time in my life.

I will always remember the first time I heard his voice. As a young teenage girl, around 15 years old, even though I did not know what I was going to say to him, I knew I needed to talk to him. I needed him in my life. The first time we talked on the phone was both scary and wonderful.

My mom and aunt set up the call, and everyone in the family knew this moment was finally going to happen for me. The call lasted about 15 minutes, but it felt like a lifetime. We talked about school and how I was doing, just small talk. He told me I could call him anytime. This was music to my ears. Finally, I had found my identity.

You see, all my life I always felt like a "misfit." No matter what I did or who I was with, I felt like I did not fit. I used to tell my mother that I did not fit with this group or that group. I did not know why, but it was always this longing inside of me to find "my place." So talking to my dad on the phone that night for the first time gave me such an internal rest and peace. I finally found him — he was a real guy.

From that night forward, we continued to talk on the phone every other week. I remember him asking me about taking Driver's Ed because he owned a car dealership, and he wanted to buy me a car. I was so excited.

Normally, our conversations would last about 30 minutes. I cannot express in words how immensely elated I was to have finally found my dad, and to find out also that I had half brothers and sisters, four to be exact.

My dad was married, and he and his wife had four children, two girls and two boys. I wanted so badly to meet them. One time I wrote my dad a letter and he wrote me back and sent a picture of them inside of it. Now, I said, I could put a face to their names.

Just being in contact with my father at this time gave me a feeling of belonging. I finally felt like I belonged, and this is something that mostly everyone desires. It brings validity to who we are, which leads to a feeling of love and acceptance. These are things, I believe, that we all crave and desire. That's what I believed, and I had finally found it!

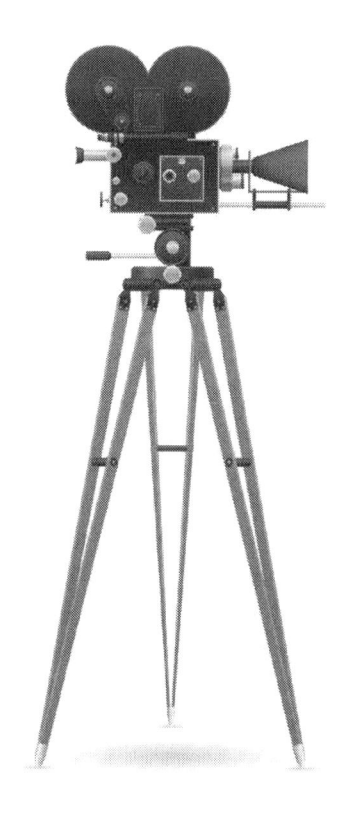

Act I Scene II: Adolescent Years

Setting: Summertime in Chicago, Illinois

Characters: Regina and Her Biological Father

After about six months of asking my mother if I could go see my Dad; she finally agreed to let me go visit him in Chicago. For years, my family would go on an annual family vacation to Las Vegas for the summer. So one summer, the same aunt who helped me find my dad drove from Chicago to Texas to visit us. I thought about it for a moment and decided this would be a great opportunity for me to beg my mother to let me go back to Chicago with my aunt to see my dad under her supervision while they go on vacation. With great trepidation, she finally agreed. So we all loaded up in her car, my aunt, a cousin, three sisters, and me and headed to Chicago.

Riding in the car with the anticipation of meeting my dad for the first time was so exciting. I could not believe it was finally going to happen. I was going to see my "real" dad in person.

When we arrived in Chicago, I stayed at my aunt's home for the first two days. I was scheduled to be there a week, but I was eager to put my arms around my dad. So the day came that she was to take me to meet him. She called to see what would be a good time to drop me off. They agreed on a time, and I couldn't wait. I was practicing my greeting, "Hi dad." "Hello, daddy." It all sounded awkward to me.

She drove me to his house, and when we arrived I nervously jumped out of the car. He greeted us at the door. There he stood, the man of my dreams. Yes, the man of my dreams. I had finally found my biological father. I often wondered what he looked like and if I had any resemblance to him.

As the door opened, I saw a five feet nine inches, caramel skin tone, medium built guy that greeted me with a hug and a somewhat weird kiss. I thought, "Wow, I've never had a man to hug me like that!" It was quite different. So we sat on the couch and watched TV, and he gave me a rundown of what the schedule would be the next morning and how my time would be spent.

I also met one of the older brothers in the family. He sat with us for a good while, and then he left and went to his room. As I sat grinning from ear to ear, I realized that one of my many dreams had come true. Afterward, my daddy took me on a brief tour of their home, which was nothing really fancy, but it was nice and adequate. It was a rustic brick home with aged furniture and stained windows that were probably caused by all of the inclement weather that Chicago experiences from year to year. Then the evening came to a close.

The dishes were put up from dinner and I was told to turn in for bed so that I would be prepared for all of the events of the following day. My father gave me another big hug and a wet kiss and sent me on my way.

I fell asleep with the next day on my mind. Well, my sleep was interrupted by what I thought was a stranger, but it was actually the voice of my dad. I got up out of bed to see what he wanted, not knowing where he was located. I walked through the house trying to find where the voice was coming from shouting, "Dad where are you?" "I'm right here," he said.

So I approached the bedroom door and walked to where he was lying in bed with the covers pulled up to his neck. I immediately wondered why he would call me into his room in the wee hours of the morning. He asked me to have a seat on the bed, being that it was so dark, I had to feel my way to the bed just to find it, and then I sat down. He began to ask me questions that seemed odd for a father who is just meeting his daughter for the first time.

"Do you have a boyfriend?"

"Have you ever kissed him?"

"Have you ever had sex before?"

I'm thinking to myself, what kind of questions are these? This was extremely weird to me and I was beginning to feel uncomfortable. So at that moment I decided to get up and go back to my room. As soon as I decided to get up, he grabbed me from behind, ripped my brand new pink pajamas so hard that a few of the buttons hit the floor. I thought to myself, "Oh no, what is he doing?"

He came out from under the covers and I was terrified because he was completely naked. I was shoved onto the bed and he began to force himself on top of me. My dad was raping me!

My heart was pounding with terror as tears were rolling down my face. I tried to scream for help, but he used his gigantic hand to cover my mouth. My lifetime short-term

> *My heart was pounding with terror as tears were rolling down my face. I tried to scream for help, but he used his gigantic hand to cover my mouth. My lifetime short-term dream had suddenly turned into a long-term nightmare.*

dream had suddenly turned into a long-term nightmare. That night, as I was fighting for my life -- to get loose from my father, truly turned out to be a *complete* disaster.

After much struggling and fighting, my father eventually got frustrated and loosened his grip slightly on me, which allowed me to fall on the floor. Then my daddy began to kick me in my stomach and back, yelling for me to get up. All I could do was crawl for my life to get to a safe place in the house. I managed to get to the nearest bathroom and lock myself in, but I was horrified just thinking of what could happen next. Needless to say, I was hysterical; I began to cry uncontrollably, not believing what had just happened.

I constantly checked the door to make sure it was still locked. I began to take the remainder of my pajamas I had on off. I was trembling like a leaf, scrubbing myself with soap and water trying to remove the filth I had just encountered. I stayed in there for what seemed like hours. I leaned up against the door, hoping and praying that he was gone. Eventually, as morning turned to dawn, I immediately rushed out of the bathroom and headed to the bedroom to get the phone number to call my aunt. Needless to say, my dad had gone into the room earlier while I was sleeping or in the bathroom and had taken all the phone numbers of my contacts in Chicago. The first thought that came to my mind was, "He has plotted to kill me." I had been set up for him to take my life. I slowly turned around and there he stood in the doorway. I'll never forget the words that came out of his mouth, "If you ever tell a soul, I'll kill you."

> *"Get your face straight," he said. So the rest of that day, I had to pretend everything was okay. That was the most difficult thing I ever had to do, but I pulled on my innate acting skills to get me through it.*

So he went in the kitchen and fixed us something to eat. He called for me to get ready because his son, David, was coming to take me touring. He knew I loved gymnastics, so he told me he was going to show me a gymnastic site that my half-sister owned.

Before David arrived to pick me up, I had to sit at the kitchen with him alone. I was so afraid. He could see that I was still upset, and he threatened me at the table again. "Get your face straight," he said. So the rest of that day, I had to pretend everything was okay. That was the most difficult thing I ever had to do, but I pulled on my innate acting skills to get me through it. I was only 15 years old, so I did not know what else to do, but this.

The whole day while trying to look poised on the outside, internally I was devastated. When we stopped to get something to eat, David ordered pizza, but I couldn't eat. He must have picked up on something because he kept asking me if everything was alright. While I wanted to tell him, nothing would come out of my mouth, but, "I'm okay."

When we finished the tour, we went back to my dad's house. Thank God, though, I was scheduled to go back to my aunt's house that night. However, my dad said he did not want to drive that late at night. I was so grateful that David chimed in and said, "I will ride with you, Dad." When we got into the car, my dad was adamant that I sit in the front seat. Once we got into the car heading to my aunt's house, his attitude changed to being nice again. Then he asked me if I wanted ice cream. I said, "No," but he said, "Yes, you do."

He pulled over to an ice cream shop and we got out of the car. As we were getting ice cream, he leaned over to me and said, "Remember, what I said." But when we got back inside the car, something rose up on the inside of me to tell David regardless. So I found something to write on and in short details, I told David what happened to me. Then I slipped the note to David on the side where my daddy could not see it. All of a sudden I heard David say, "Oh my God!" I knew he had gotten the message and I felt somewhat free.

Then the car went bumpy bump turning off the road suddenly in a jerking motion. I knew then my dad was going to kill me. I knew he knew that I had just told David about what he had done. At that moment, I didn't know whether or not I was going to make it out alive. I guessed my dad figured out through David's, "Oh my God," that I told him.

He turned the steering wheel onto a gravel dirt area, slowly proceeding to drive. My heart felt like it was coming out of my chest and I couldn't breathe. I kept my head down because I did not know what was going to happen next. Then I looked up, it was actually the road leading to my aunt's house. Oh...what a sigh of relief I felt. But even though I was relieved, I was still trembling inside. I was frightened "out of my wits," and my adrenaline was flowing at a maximum level.

Finally, we reached my aunt's house, and my daddy went in the house to talk to my aunt, but David and I went for a walk. We talked, hugged and cried for about 30 minutes. David was only in his early twenties, and he really did not know what to do. But that night, he showed himself to be a friend and a confidant. As we parted, he wanted us to stay in touch and he gave me his phone number. So that night when they left, I knew I would never see my daddy again. After waiting fifteen years to meet my real daddy, it took only moments to lose him for the rest of my life.

The next morning, my cousin who rode with me, also noticed that something was wrong. Of course initially, I said there was nothing wrong. But he kept saying, "I know there is something wrong." Eventually, I told him what happened and he told my aunt. I told them both, it was okay, so don't worry about it.

But when I returned home, three days later, the weirdest thing happened. The headline on the newspaper on the table at my mom's house read, **"Dad Rapes Teenage Girl!"** "OH MY GOD," I thought. Who did I tell that works at the newspaper company? I begin to panic! I thought my dad might think I told them. I was afraid he was finally going to attempt what he set out to do, kill me. But I never saw him again nor did my parents notice anything was wrong with me.

However, within a week after this incident, I told one of my half-sisters. I told her everything. Then she told her daddy, who was my mother's current husband. When they heard about it, they were on vacation in California. My mother was belligerent! She was so enraged when she found out. She wanted to kill my daddy. She called and got him on the telephone and asked, "If he knew the meaning of death," because he was a dead man.

My parents could not come back from vacation fast enough. When they got back home, she took me into a room by myself, and we hugged and cried. I will never forget this moment. My mother apologized profusely and told me how much she was sorry it happened. And from time to time after this, when I wanted to talk about this incident or other things that might bother me, she would just listen. My mother was always encouraging and she wanted me to know that this situation did not define me. Now, everything was out in the open. However, IT WAS NOT OVER!

INTERMISSION

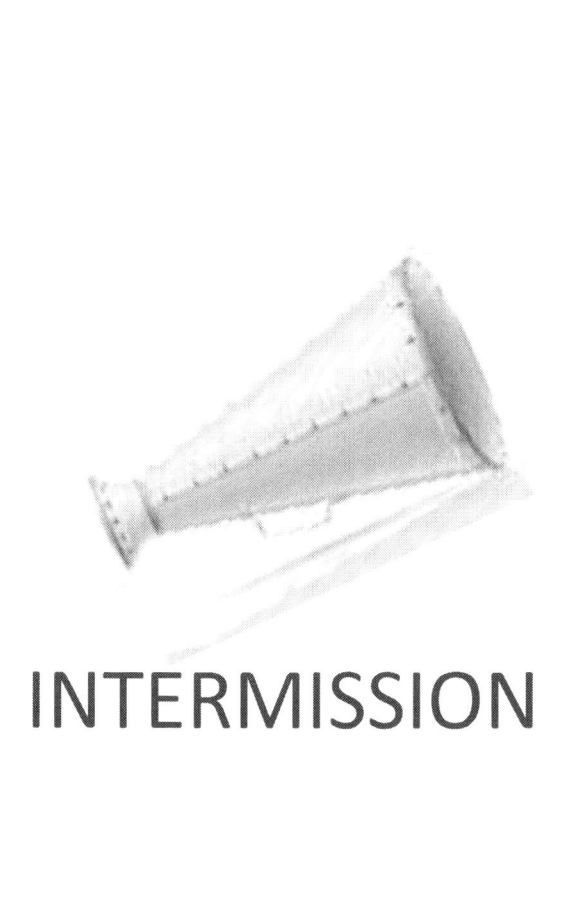

REFLECTION

If you feel in any way that the script of your life has been altered by untrained actors/actresses, pray and ask God to go with you in the theatre of your mind, so you can revisit the sensitive areas in the script of your life. We can't conquer those things we are not willing to confront. It's critical that you get dominion over it before it infiltrates every area of your life.

Dear Lord,

You are the Head of my life, and You know all about me. Many things have transpired in my life that I have just swept under the rug, never to visit again. It's those very things that continue to haunt me throughout my adult life. I'm asking You to help me face those things that have blocked me from being who You created me to be. Please be with me, and give me the courage as I face these giants. In Jesus Name I pray, AMEN.

Act I Scene III: My High School Years
                Revisit the Script

Setting: Various Locations

Characters: Regina, High School Students
               and Undisclosed Others

After the incident with my dad, I thought this might perhaps be a temporary nightmare. However, it was not. During my high school years, this really affected my life and my mental stamina. Even though I was a cheerleader, student council member, honor student, gymnastics team member; I struggled constantly with the horror of that night. And at times, my conscious and my memory got the best of me. I found myself saying, "Well, so much for that!" I found myself thinking, "What is the point of trying to be good when someone has just taken my virginity." You see, all my life my mother told me to save myself for marriage. And just thinking about this drove me to a place of what seemed like a place of no return at times.

Let me interrupt this scene for a moment. Parents, while it is important for us to teach our daughters to save themselves, and to remain pure, it is also important that we allow them to know that if something ever happens, or they mess up, that they can begin again. They are not soiled indefinitely. They still are invaluable precious jewels with a purpose in the Kingdom.

Like many of us, we try to consume ourselves with other things to help cover up the hurt and pain in our hearts. This was the reason I was involved in so many activities. I was determined to block out of my mind what had happened to me. Looking back, it was probably the worst thing I could have done. But all the competitions that I was in as a gymnast and all the school games I cheered at could not drown out my own subconscious.

I was a great gymnast. I started gymnastics classes while in elementary school. I remember forging my mother's name on the application permission form just to be a part. However, this was the turning point in my life. In many ways, it did help me stay focus, but in many ways, it was not the solution. But I enjoyed it and I got to compete quite a bit.

My mother did not attend the majority of my gymnastics competitions. She was always afraid that I was going to get hurt, but no matter what I did or how much I competed, none of it could keep me from my own internal thoughts and nightmares.

Looking back on everything now, I have come to realize that when you keep something in the dark and try to handle it on your own, the devil will always use it to bring chaos into your life as well as alter your mindset. What the devil does is take the secret areas of your life and taunt you with them, which is one of his specialties. This is what I endured. Because I kept this secret pretty much to myself, the devil taunted and haunted me with the memories for years.

You see, the devil's intent is to infiltrate your mind to render you helpless causing you to be incapable of making sound decisions. But the enemy knows that once the chains are broken off your life and you get revelation of who God is and who you really are, your past cannot hold you back; people can't control you; and your problems won't be able to shake you because your present will be an indication that Almighty God is working in you.

When negative seeds are planted in your life, know that these seeds are a part of the devil's plan to defeat you. If you give attention to these seeds, the devil will release a harvest in your life based on these negative seeds. And what he wants is for those negative seeds to rise up and strangle the very life from various areas in your life.

It is evident that this is what he did in my life. And let me say this, back then counseling was not an option. I didn't have money for it, nor was I going to ask my mother; internalizing it was my only means of therapy.

So over time, this secret pain drove me to a place of what I thought was no return. I became very angry inside, hating all people and all things. I was this awesome student by day, involved in everything I could be in, and an amazing sinner by night. I started experimenting with all kinds of things. I would think to myself, I have to find a way to stop this pain. I have to stop it!

I was constantly fighting and provoking fights in my neighborhood with guys and girls. I just did not fit in with the "cliques." Nor did I really understand back then why I was fighting so much. Today, I can understand this stage in my life, but this was just the beginning.

When my biological father raped me, I became so detached emotionally from my family. It was nothing they did, but it felt like everyone heard about what happened and all eyes were on me. There was a level of shame that I couldn't put into words. These were the years I also started experimenting with drugs: cocaine, marijuana, speed, etc. Whatever I could get my hands on, I tried it. This was the beginning of a long protracted time of me using drugs. All the years I did drugs, my mother never knew it. Perhaps, it was because I was so active in afterschool activities, but in high school I especially used "speed" to keep me pumped up so I could function well as a cheerleader.

I was a cheerleader from my sophomore through my senior year in high school. The school was predominately "white." My cousin and I were the only African-American girls on the squad. Therefore, we had to be the best.

When you experience life-altering events, you try to change who you are. You try to become something or someone different because being who you are provokes painful memories. This is what I went through during these years.

Often I found myself in the theatrical dressing room of my mind constantly switching outfits into something that made me feel better. However, the most drastic part of the outfit change was the mask. I wore a mask so that people would not be able to see the real me. I didn't want anyone to know the person who was hurting so badly. I figured I could disguise myself and become someone else. Maybe in doing this, the new person could get rid of the hurt person inside of me.

THE MASK

Don't Be Fooled By Me

Don't be fooled by me,

Don't be fooled by the face I wear, for

I wear a mask,

A thousand masks, masks that I am

afraid to take off, and none of them is

me.

Pretending is an art that's second

nature with me,

But don't be fooled; for God's sake

don't be fooled.

I give you the impression that I'm

secure, that all is sunny and unruffled

with me,

Within as well as without,

That confidence is my name and

coolness my game,

That the water's calm and I'm in

command, and that I need no one, but

don't believe me.

My surface may seem smooth, but my

surface is my mask,

Ever-varying and ever-concealing,

beneath lies no complacency.

Beneath lies confusion, fear, and

aloneness. But I hide this.

I don't want anyone to know it; I panic at the thought of my weakness being exposed.

That's why I frantically create a mask to hide behind, a nonchalant sophisticated façade, to help me pretend, to shield me from the glance that knows.

But such a glance is precisely my salvation, my only hope, and I know it.

That is, if it's followed by acceptance, if it's followed by love.

It's the only thing that can liberate me from myself,

from my own self-built prison walls,

from the barriers I so painfully erect.

It's the only thing that will assure me

of what I can't assure myself, that I'm

really worth something.

But I don't tell you this. I don't dare

to. I'm afraid to.

I'm afraid you'll think less of me, that

you'll laugh,

And your laugh would kill me. I'm

afraid that deep down I'm nothing

And that you will see this and reject

me.

--Anonymous

INTERMISSION

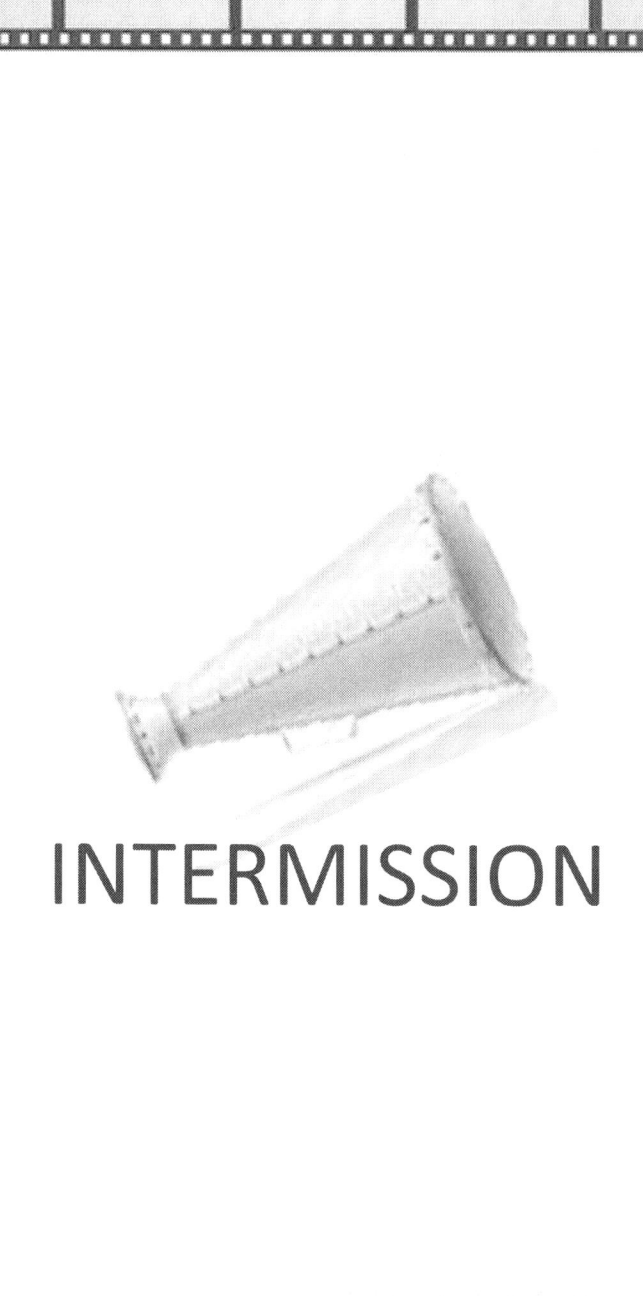

Now, on with the production...

In the book of Ephesians, we find God has predestined us and chosen us to spend eternity with Him. He has placed a deposit in each of us guaranteeing us a role in His final production. And it is crucial that you and I are willing to carry out the assignment, or shall I say our part, in the Production. Perhaps, you might ask, "What is my part?"

Your part is to actively participate by taking control of the script you were given and cause it to come alive. Why? There are people's lives at stake and their deliverance is dependent upon your ability to get through the challenges of your life story. This

> *Your pain is your platform to bring hope to the hopeless and your part is so critical, because someone is waiting to see your final production.*

can seem difficult because many people are ashamed of their past and their present state because they don't understand it; therefore, they are more concerned about their future.

Whatever has transpired in your life is the very reason for your existence. I heard someone say, "Your mess is your message." Your pain is your platform to bring hope to the hopeless and your part is so critical, because someone is waiting to see your final production. You must realize there is hope in unfavorable situations.

Here, you have "The Producer and The Performer" of all times. And because you are like Him, you have been given that same power to create and set the stage of your life. But you must first, within the theatre of your mind, ask yourself, "What would I like to see or experience at this point in my life?" Secondly, take those thoughts and begin to speak into existence what you see. Thirdly, begin to act upon what you see. You have been given the creative ability to script your performance.

The time is now!

"Take delight in the Lord, and He will give you the desires of your heart" (Psalm 37:4 NIV)

Here are some questions you can ask yourself:

- What is my assignment?
- What do I see?
- What do I want to experience at this stage in my life?

Remember, this is your script.

If you feel in any way that your script has been altered, pray and ask God to assist you in revisiting the script of your life.

When I say revisit the script, I mean to look over the script of your life story and look for the parts you want to keep and use to enhance your production. Keep in mind, God doesn't waste anything. I heard one person say, that God is a very "economical God." This means that He doesn't waste *anything* good, bad or indifferent. Instead He uses it all for your good.

Now, at this point, you need to:

- First, take a good look at what has happened over the course of your life.

- Second, evaluate consistent patterns both good and bad.

- Third, decide what adjustments are necessary in order to have a more favorable outcome.

Act II Scene I: Getting It Together

Setting: College Years in Various Locations

Characters: Regina and Undisclosed Others

Many times we try to do things outside of our character to prevent us from feeling hurt. We begin to act out in ways that we generally wouldn't if we were not trying to be someone we are not. For instance, during my college years. It seemed as though everything started to turn from bad to worse. I acted out roles in the production of my life that I was not authorized to be playing. Illegal drugs were definitely my companion in college. I experimented with all types of drugs and alcohol as I stated earlier. Truly, there was probably not a drug that I did not try (Opium,

PCP, heroin, uppers, downers, etc.). I was completely out of control. I look back now on how involved I was in drugs, and it's hard for me to believe that I don't have some form of brain damage.

> *When things are this out of control, you might find yourself being upset with God, wondering why He would allow such bad things to happen to you.*

When things are this out of control, you might find yourself being upset with God, wondering why He would allow such bad things to happen to you. I didn't grow up in the church, so realizing that God allows dramatic things to strengthen us was foreign to me.

Wow, who would think that going through something so horrible was supposed to strengthen you and bring you perseverance? But it is clearly stated in James 1:2-4, "Consider it pure joy, my brothers and sisters, whenever you face trials of any kinds, because you know that the testing of your faith produces perseverance. Let perseverance finish its work so that you may be mature and complete, not lacking anything."

During my college years, you can say, "I was a girl gone wild!" I partied so much my first year in college that I almost flunked out. Then I realized I had only two options: Get it together or go back home. And since I did not want to go back home, my only option was to get it together. So I did – a little!

You see, my mother was a stickler for me getting my degree. She wanted to make sure I would be properly prepared to take care of myself in life. Plus, she knew the value of education. All throughout her schooling she had wonderful teachers who got behind her and encouraged her to continue her education. In fact, it was her English teacher that did the paperwork for her to go to college. She believed in her so much that she went the extra mile for my mother to make it. She was even able to get a full scholarship for her at Wiley College, but my mom did not want to go to this college. So she chose to go to a college in Chicago. At the first college she attended, there were only nine blacks on the campus. After completing the first year, she switched to another college in an adjacent county. So not getting my degree was not an option for me.

However, I continued to do drugs, but regardless of all the drugs, I was still involved in extra-curricular activities. One of the activities I really enjoyed was dancing. I competed in dance contests and in one of them I came in second place. I remember being so excited about one competition because there were celebrity judges. It was a great time in my life.

It is funny how God works and thinks. Right when we think we are getting things all together, doing things our own way, God allows the script to be flipped a little again. I have not always understood why He did this, but I know now this is just His way of reminding us that He is still in control. He is a master of allowing different actors into your life at odd times. He would allow a script change or a rewrite anytime.

The script switched on me early in my college years. Actually, it was a totally unexpected character that showed up on the scene.

I went home to visit and was asked to babysit a relative's child. This particular evening, I decided to spend the night since they weren't going to return until the wee hours of the

> *I fell asleep, only to be awakened by someone standing over me with just his underwear on..."Oh no, could this be happening to me again?"..."I am being raped a second time."*

morning. I put the kids to bed and made myself comfortable on the couch. Soon after this, I fell asleep, only to be awakened by someone standing over me wearing only his underwear. I jumped up fearing who it was because I couldn't see due to the darkness. Then suddenly I was grabbed and my mouth was muffled as the vision of the person became clearer. "Oh no, could this be happening to me again?" I thought frantically in my mind, "I am being raped a second time." I was so much in a state of shock that I could not yell. The only thing that was coming to my mind was what my biological father said to me, "If you say anything, I will kill you." I was so afraid for my life AGAIN!

Fear is one of the most effective tools in the devil's arsenal. When we allow ourselves to be crippled by fear, once a seed has been planted and germinated, it will continue to grow out of control until we deal with it. Fear for my life, prevented me from telling anyone what had happened with my father. Fear of not being believed, prevented me from telling as well.

Fear is a root that grows deep and is hard to remove; the longer it is allowed to grow. 2 Timothy 1:7 says, *"For God has not given us a spirit of fear, but of power, and love and of a sound mind."* So we know that when we have a harvest of fear in our lives, it is the enemy's way of keeping us immobilized so that we will not fulfill our destiny in life.

> *The tactic of the devil is, if he can just keep us quiet, therefore, these areas in our lives can haunt us for months and even years.*

One thing that I now realize is that holding everything in was a major scene change for me. The enemy takes those things that we keep hidden and uses them to shut us down. The tactic of the devil is to keep us muzzled so that these areas in our lives can haunt us for months and even years. What we have to realize is stated very eloquently in Ephesians 6:10-18 (NIV): *"Finally, be strong in the Lord and in his mighty power. Put on the full armor of God, so that you can take your stand against the devil's schemes. For our struggle is not against flesh and blood, but against the rulers, against the authorities, against the powers of this dark world and against the spiritual forces of evil in the heavenly realms. Therefore put on the full armor of God, so that when the day of evil comes, you may be able to stand your ground, and after you have done everything, to stand. Stand firm then, with the belt of truth buckled around your waist, with the readiness that comes from the gospel of peace. In addition to all this, take up the shield of faith, with which you can extinguish all the flaming arrows of the evil one. Take the helmet of salvation and the sword of the Spirit, which is the word of God. And pray in the Spirit on all occasions with all kinds of prayers and requests. With this in mind, be alert and always keep on praying for all the Lord's people."*

Holding things in is just another way we continue to wear the mask of who we really are NOT. We need to head back into the dressing rooms of our lives and take the mask off.

So, the next day I shared with my parents what had transpired and they were livid. They both were in shock and couldn't believe as a family we were faced with this again. As with most parents, some things are beyond their ability to handle, but they addressed the matter with the accused and put measures in place to make certain that I wouldn't be placed in that position again.

> *Holding things in is just another way we continue to wear the mask of who we really are NOT.*

Even with that assurance, I still felt uneasy as if I didn't know who I was. I'm sure you've felt this feeling of hopelessness before. You ask questions to yourself like, "Why me, Lord? What did I do to deserve this?" Then you go through life pretending to be someone you are not to cope.

Act II Scene II: Delivered, But Not Free

Setting: Various Locations

Characters: Regina's Mother, the Holy Spirit, Undisclosed Others and Dr. Regina Spellmon

As this masquerade went on, I kept the mask on for several more years. I had different ways that I would find myself acting out. I had been hurt so by men that my goal back then was to hurt them the way they hurt me. I would set up sex rendezvous and right when I was about to have sex, I would leave them hanging. This went on for a while, and then I met a man who eventually became my husband.

Initially, when I met this guy, yes, he was good looking, but dating was not on my mind, at least not having any serious relationships. And trust me; he had more of his share of women wanting to date him. However, I was not one of them.

For two years, from the time we met during our freshman year in college, we were just friends. Of course, I ran into him all the time on campus. Even though I knew he was somewhat interested in me, I never wanted to date him. It was my junior year in college that we started dating.

I am not sure the actual moment we started dating because we had known each other so long, but the relationship definitely changed in our junior year. We started spending more time together. We started attending school activities and football games together. We spent most of our free time together. We didn't make "A's" and "B's" in all of our courses, but we passed them all.

We also spent a lot of time visiting family and friends. We would go out to eat at restaurants or he would cook for me. Some nights we would stay up all night talking and having a good time. Upon graduation from North Texas State University with a Bachelor of Science Degree in Community Health Education, and a minor in Biology and Physical Education, it was inevitable we were going to get married.

I often comment on the fact that this is something I had to do because my mom jokingly told me I couldn't come back home if I didn't get my degree. I laugh about it now, but it was quite serious back then. It was serious because I had to continue doing and being someone I wasn't. Remember, I was still struggling with my self-worth and significance after being raped two times. I never told my boyfriend about this, but there was always this dark place or hole that I could not fulfill.

We talked about getting married, so when he asked me to marry him, I was extremely excited. Of course, I said, yes. I graduated in December 1982, and we married on January 8, 1983. He got a job in Houston, TX and this city became our home.

I hated Houston! It was very difficult for me to find work and I was extremely miserable. After living there for about a year and a half, we moved to Fort Worth, TX -- my hometown. By the time we moved to Fort Worth, TX, I had gotten a job at the same company with my husband. We were transferred to an office in Dallas, TX. We were thrilled because the company offered us a full relocation package.

After moving to Fort Worth and working with the company for a short time, I wanted to do something else. After all, I just wanted to get on with the company for the extra money. I started looking around for suitable jobs for me and I applied to be a substitute teacher. I was hired as a substitute teacher, but it was not long that I grew weary of doing that.

By this time, my mom had resigned from the Post Office and started a business – Floral Arrangement Service. She was quite talented in this area. She had contracts for weddings, offices, homes, and all sorts of events. After hearing my desire to do something else, she encouraged me to learn the floral business. I thought about it for a little while, and then I decided to go head and join her in the business. Eventually, we became such a power team of entrepreneurs that we opened up another business. We talked and strategized about what we could do to expand and we decided to open up a salon/shop.

Mom went to nail school for four weeks while I ran the business. Then I went to beauty school for nine months to learn the trade and she ran the business. We had lots of customers and the money was good. We did so well that we opened up another salon on the other side of town.

Let me say this right here. When I started working with my mother and doing business with her, I did not know the Lord. He was not a part of our equation. I was also never totally healed from my past, but our newfound success kept me from dwelling on it. Therefore, I felt I had arrived. But God knows our time and our turn.

Well, my time and turn came on a New Year's Eve night.

Months (maybe even years), there was a small voice that stayed inside my head pushing me to really search deep inside for my purpose. I was married and it was going well. I had a good job, everything was going good, but something was still missing. I still had voids that drugs or alcohol could not fill.

Then one dark cold night, New Year's Eve to be exact, I was driving around in a brand new Mercedes Benz, high as a kite when "out of the blue," my car broke down. When I looked up it had stopped directly in front of a church. I got out of the car and stumbled inside trying to find help for my car. I walked into this old white building where it was very warm on the inside. All I remember is that the floor was covered with red carpet that led into the sanctuary. I followed the path and opened two large doors and began to holler out for help.

"Hello, Hello...is anyone here?"

Then I heard a voice of a man that responded, "Hi, may I help you?"

"Yes sir, my car stopped outside in front of the church and I need to see if someone can help me start it?"

"I can see what's going on with your car, but first let me ask you ma'am, do you know Jesus?"

"Who? Sir I just need my car fixed so I can get home. Is there anybody else here that can help, if you can't help me?"

"Ma'am, I can help you, but first, I would like to know if you know Jesus?" He repeated.

At that point I was starting to get upset. First of all, I was "high" and my "high" was leaving with all those questions he was asking me. Secondly, I was trying to get to the party that I was heading to when my car stopped. So I decided to appease him so I could get back to where I was headed in the first place.

"No sir, I don't know Jesus, who is He?" I asked reluctantly.

He responded with, "He is the One who can mend your broken heart."

"But my heart isn't broken, it's my car that needs help, sir" I smirked.

> *By the time all of this was said and done, I was in tears. I had fallen to the floor and was crying like I had just lost a loved one...That night I was saved.*

"Let me pray with you and then we can get your car fixed. Please repeat after me. Lord, I know I am a sinner..."

"Lord I know I am a sinner..." I repeated with uncertainty.

By the time all of this was said and done, I was in tears. I had fallen to the floor and was crying like I had just lost a loved one. When I finally got myself together; the man had left. So I decided to sneak back to my car to keep from facing him again, and wouldn't you know as soon as I got in and closed the door, the car started right up!

That night I was saved.

My "high" was gone, and I ended up not going to the party after all. Initially, I was mad he messed up my "high," but God saved my soul that night.

It was right around that time that I felt the presence of God and I came across a scripture that was very profound to me: *"You, dear children, are from God and have overcome them, because the one who is in you is greater than the one who is in the world"* (1 John 4:4).

I finally began to feel that maybe I did have purpose after all...and that was a pretty good feeling. The next morning I woke up, I could not believe what had happened to me the night before. Was I dreaming? Did I make all this up in my head? Was the whole episode real from last night? Regardless of what I thought, I knew something had drastically changed on the inside of me.

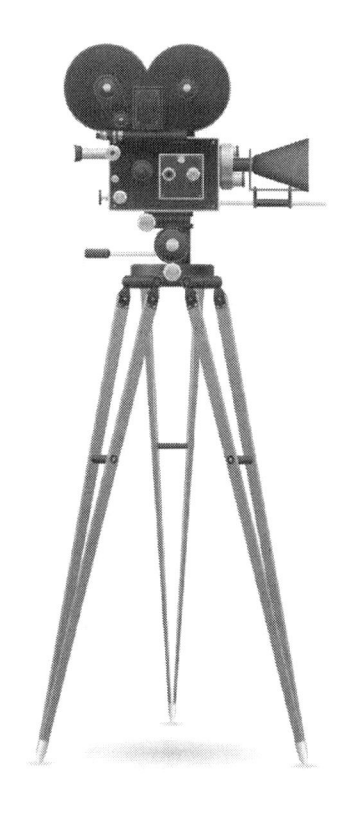

Act II Scene III: This is Not What I Had in Mind

Setting: Various Locations

Characters: Dr. Regina Spellmon, Her Family and Undisclosed Others

Have you ever experienced a time when you really felt God's presence in your life? Things are going well for you and you are on top of the world? This is where I was at this point in my life. After praying the sinner's prayer that night with the pastor in that church, my life radically changed.

I started attending church. I got involved with community activities. I really enjoyed my newfound life in Christ. My mom was saved. My husband was saved, and I had gotten through all of the drama in my life. My life was finally on an upswing. So much so that God told me to let everything go. I knew what He meant. He wanted me to walk away from the businesses we had opened up. This was in 1989 when He spoke this to me. When I told my mother, she did not try to convince me not to do it. She believed I was hearing from God, and she was at peace with my decision.

> *When I gave the businesses up, I really did not know exactly what God had for me at this time in my life. All I knew, He was telling me to let it go.*

When I gave up the businesses, I really did not know exactly what God wanted me to do at this time in my life. All I knew, He was telling me to let it all go. My husband and I sought God for His direction, and eventually He spoke to our spirit to start a church, and we did.

We started a church in Fort Worth, TX, and we named it Ambassadors of Christ Christian Center. My husband was the Pastor and I was the Co-Pastor. The church eventually became one of the largest churches in Fort Worth. It was well known in the community for its creativity and excitement. We started a school and taught many of the children in Fort Worth and the surrounding cities. The school went from Pre-K to 12th grade. We originated dance teams, football teams, cheerleading teams, praise teams, you name it. It was happening at Ambassadors. I was also the youth pastor, so my life was wonderful.

I thought......until another actor interrupted my life.

For years, my husband and I had a friend, who was a Christian, and we knew him very well. I might say, he and my husband were very close. He lived in another city with his wife. One day we decided to take a break and go out of town in the city they lived in. We had to stay overnight in the city, where our Christian friend lived, so my husband called and asked if we could stay in their home. Of course, they had no problem with it, but they had only a limited amount of sleeping beds.

When my husband mentioned this to me earlier, I really did not want to stay at someone else's home. I practically begged him to go to a hotel. I just felt we needed to do this. But with the continual prompting of my husband, eventually I gave in and agreed to the arrangements.

We had a great time at our friends' home, and then the men went into another room to watch sports games. As the hour grew late, I bedded on the sofa out front. The men fell asleep in the room watching television and his wife went to her room to sleep. But I had no idea what that night had in store for me.

"Don't you say a word," are the words I heard after being startled from my deep sleep. All I could see was the silhouette of my husband's friend's body lunged over me, while his hands covered my nose and mouth. As I became coherent to what was happening to me, I begin to fight back. But no matter how much I struggled and fought, I became a victim of rape again. I could not believe I was in this same situation for the third time. But this time I was saved. So why was I being raped. I was no longer a sinner; I was a pastor's wife.

After it was all over, I stayed awake the remainder of the night. I could not wait until the morning, so we could leave. I was so traumatized and trapped in my mental cage from the first two rapes; I couldn't tell anybody, not even my husband. I just kept silent. The next morning we woke up, we got dressed, went home and went to church. I thought I was okay...but I was not.

One of the things I noticed was that I was angry at my husband for not protecting me. I felt like it was his fault to a degree. I wanted to stay in a hotel, but he insisted that we stay with them. I know some might be wondering why I did not tell my husband. It was something about them being so close and all that I had been through in the past that kept me from saying anything. It was a weird thing and a weird era in my life. I never thought about calling the police either.

> *There was no past behavior or odd proclivities that registered in my mind that he would do such a thing. He raped a FIRST LADY – a co-pastor of a church, and he was supposed to be a Christian.*

My husband and I knew this friend for over 10 years, and by this time we had been pastoring for a period of some years, so there was no past behavior or odd proclivities that registered in my mind that he would do such a thing. He raped a FIRST LADY – a Co-Pastor of a church, and he was supposed to be a Christian as well. Today, I thank God for the church because when I look back on this period in my life, I realized the "church" saved me. I had to "Faith It" until I "Made It."

By this time, our congregation had grown to about 300 to 400 members. But in a matter of a few additional years, it grew to about 1,000 people. And it continued to grow, and so did my family. We had a child placed into our care, who we raised as our own. She became the joy of my life. There were many challenges early on, but I must say it was worth it. I wouldn't trade her for the world. I have a granddaughter that I call my own and a grandson that has recently "popped up" on the scene. Although I never had kids of my own, I have always held a special place in my heart for them.

There is an old adage that says, "To whom much is given much is required." With our congregation growing so large, there was a greater amount of responsibility that came with a ministry of this magnitude. So I felt the need early on to continue my education. I figured it would prepare me for what was ahead. I graduated from Southwestern Baptist Theological Seminary with a Masters of Divinity Degree. I call that my doctorate, because it took me five long hard years to complete it due to the prejudices I encountered being female and black. It was very difficult. My Doctorate in Theology took only two years. I've always felt that if every other profession requires schooling, surely the ministers of the gospel should be required to do the same.

We constantly had to take care of things to maintain a level of excellence in ministry. Our church was such a cutting edge church that it was viewed as the premier church in the community for innovation and ingenuity. And boy, we were working hard to keep up with the growth! But eventually the "growing pains" caught up with us. While we looked picture perfect on the outside, internally, every day, we were striving hard to secure our existence. No matter how hard we worked, "the walls came tumbling down."

The picture perfect tapestry had flaws, and when it started unraveling, it unraveled so fast until every aspect of the ministry and personal lives came apart. As I think back on it now, it is truly true what the Bible says, "Pride goes before a fall."

It was like we had a mindset that we had arrived. I am not saying I was completely innocent in all of this, but when God began to show me this, I realized I was becoming somebody I was not. But there was a consistent, unspoken pressure that I needed to conform to somebody else's standards to be accepted.

Well, our "perfect" ministry and our "perfect" marriage and our "perfect" family fell apart. One by one everything turned into a "perfect" disaster. The joint ministry that my husband and I shared became my baby. I was given the choice by God, "Obey and pastor this church" or run and hide. I wanted to run, hide and leave the state, but God would not let me. There were members, who were loyal and true, but it was hard to differentiate between the two, so I felt alone. Yes, there were issues on both parts in the marriage, but there were so many other challenges we had to endure regarding our personal life and the ministry.

Number One, I did not plan on being a single parent and grandmother. Two, I did not plan on being totally responsible for the growth and spiritual care for a congregation, while I tried to tend to my own personal wounds. This was certainly not my idea of a good time, and I almost resented God for making me choose what I knew I had to choose.

In a way, it was like the shock of being RAPED all over again. Rape is often associated with a physical sexual act, but it can actually occur in someone mentally, spiritually and emotionally. Throughout my life, I believe I have been raped in every way possible.

But this time, it was different. This time I faced my perpetrators, one by one as they came up against me.

But this time, it was different. This time I faced my perpetrators, one by one as they came up against me. I stood up for myself. I held my head high. Although trembling through it all, I fought back. I continued pastoring what was left of the church. I continued to do what I was called to do, in spite of the pain I was feeling. I cannot pretend it was easy. I cannot pretend I did not cry. I cannot pretend anything because it was one of the most difficult times in my life.

Yes, my marriage ended in divorce. Yes, we lost the church building. Yes, we lost the gorgeous home we were living in. Yes, I lost the car I was driving. Yes, most of our church members left. Yes, I eventually became homeless by choice. But God!!! And because I was willing to face the enemy head on, God was there and He knocked each one of them down, one by one and restored all.

God could have done this for me throughout my history of rapes, but I was afraid during those years, and hiding was my choice of action. One thing I know for sure now, God does not give us the spirit of fear. But just like faith is an effective tool to bring about positive results, fear is an effective tool to bring about negative results.

Fear can physically, mentally, emotionally and even spiritually paralyze us and hinder us from forging ahead to see what the end results will be. We cannot move, not because we don't want to move, but because we are too afraid to move. The paralysis occurs because we focus more on the event, which causes fear to tie us up. When we face that thing that wants to hinder us, and knock us down, it opens a path whereby we are able to move forward. I often say, "When we can get under what is over us, we can get over what is under us," this is a statement coined by an incredible pastor in the 21st Century, Ed Young.

It sounds a bit confusing, but dissecting the issue, can bring clarity. When we get under who is over us -- God, we can get over the things that try to light a fire beneath us. Getting ourselves aligned properly with God gives us the strength to get pass and over the things that want to trip us up or stop us in life. Makes more sense doesn't it? Line yourself up correctly with God and you will have a smoother journey. It is kind of like getting your car aligned. In order to have the smoothest ride possible, you have to get your car aligned from time to time. Without this alignment you will find yourself veering to the right or to the left.

Experiencing the things I went through in my life, prepared me, empowered me, strengthened me, and enabled me to carry out the calling God had for me.

Jeremiah 29:11 says, *"For I know the plans I have for you, says the Lord, plans to prosper and not harm you."* This verse can seem contradictory as we live through the "plans" God seems to have for us. How can being raped, by someone you should be able to trust be in God's plans for me to prosper? How can God turn my mess of a life into something that doesn't harm me? As I said before, while going through it, it did hurt, but the amazing thing about God is that He can take what we think is the hardest, most horrific, most ugly things we face in life, and use those very same things to our benefit later in life. He uses the strength we get from going through situations and unwanted scenes in our scripts to propel us into our next scene, as well as sustain us while we are going through challenges. Had we not grown through the last scene, we would not be able to exist in the next scene. "Destiny does not come **without** disruptions," says Bishop T. D. Jakes, a tremendous preacher and teacher in the 21st century.

Trust the "Author" of your story; don't get stuck on the current scene. We have to learn to trust God all the way. The Bible says, *"Trust in the Lord with all your heart, and lean not unto your own understanding, but in ALL your ways acknowledge Him and He shall direct your paths"* (Proverbs 3:5-6). Some versions even say "make your paths straight." That means don't get stuck gazing at the scenery or the props, or even the actors in the current scene, just trust the One who wrote the story. "All" sometimes is bigger than it seems. "All" includes your current seemingly unlivable situation. It includes things big and small. It includes anything that may not make sense to you, as you view the current scene that you are experiencing. So trust God with ALL of your "alls," and He shall make your paths straight.

When you drive from Texas to California you drive through some of the most dull, non-beautiful scenes you can imagine. I mean seriously, how many cactus and sand-filled scenes can you admire? When you climb the altitudes of the mountains, you wonder "will I ever reach the top before my ears pop?" When you are traveling back down the other side and the road curves around and around, your mind wonders, "What am I doing, where am I going, and will I ever get there?" BUT when you get to the Pacific Coast highway and see the spacious, most glorious sight of the ocean being itself, it is beyond amazing. You could have stopped any place and time during that trip, and you would have cheated yourself out of the final scene. And it is the same way with life. You don't always see the other side when you are going through difficult times, but if you would persevere, the light will shine on the other side.

I encourage you that no matter where you are in your production trust the Play Writer. Don't get distracted by the people, places or things you encounter, instead trust the One who has the knowledge of every scene you will encounter and enjoy what He has prepared for you.

Yes, I was raped three times in my life. But God used my ordeal to restore many ladies back to wholeness and He is still doing it. Before the church went through its demise, the Lord allowed me to design a program call, "SACRED," which stood for "Sexually Abused Children Reaching Emotional Dominion." There were so many ladies that attended this event from our church and also from the community that I counseled who had been raped or sexually abused that we started this program to walk them through their deliverance. We had a licensed counselor working with us and some other incredible volunteers to assist us with this endeavor. As well, we created many partnerships with businesses such as hair stylists, limo services, make-up artists, whatever we needed to build up the ladies' self-esteem.

Also, God took care of my basic needs. He gave me a Mercedes Benz that I did not ask for or pursue. It was a supernatural favor that God spoke to a man's heart to work out for me. Again, I did not ask for it or seek it. It was all God's doing. Besides, because of all the debt we incurred with the building, the losing of our home, my credit was "shot." I couldn't get approval for anything.

Also, I am staying in a better living situation. When my husband and I lost our 5,000 square feet home, we moved to an apartment. And not long after this, I decided to leave. I wasn't sure where I was going to go; then my mother reminded me of a rental property that was in the family, so I eventually made my abode there. There was no hot water initially when I moved in, so I had to take cold showers. But my living

> *Sometimes, not having all the basic needs are better than not having peace.*

situation has changed for the better as well. Sometimes, it is better to have peace than having all of your basic needs met without peace.

And lastly, God has restored our church membership and our building. We literally got down to 25 to 30 members and in about six years, God has given us about 300 members on the roster. Now, we have a new facility, and we are growing steadily. Right now, we are expanding our existing building to accommodate even more growth. It is a thriving healthy work and people are being made whole, not perfect, but "whole."

As I look back on what God has brought me through, and how He has orchestrated the affairs of my life, I am truly grateful. He has taken the PIECES of my life and put me back together according to His liking. Now, I have PEACE – the peace that surpasses all understanding. He has truly taken me FROM PIECES TO PEACE!

And, if you are still wondering, "How peace is possible when life feels like it has been running you over like a freight train." I want you to know once and for all, peace is possible. In the midst of your storm, if you will trust God and focus on the Savior and not what you need to be saved from, He will give you peace. In John 16:33 according to the Message Bible Jesus tells us, *"I've told you all this so that trusting me, you will be unshakable and assured, deeply at peace. In this godless world you will continue to experience difficulties. But take heart! I've conquered the world!"*

I have had many opportunities to just curl up in a ball and give up. Maybe even look up and say to God, "Why have you forsaken me?" Then I think of what Jesus endured when the people closest to Him turned their backs on Him in His darkest hour. You may feel like the people closest to you have turned their backs on you, or maybe you feel like you have had a few friends like Judas who sold you out for their own benefit. Knowing what Jesus went through, lets you know that He thought well of you and that you were worth His own wounds.

I have been hurt so many times that I started to expect it. Then I ended up hurting myself by pushing the people who did love me away. I encourage you to find a scripture that speaks to your heart. Something that you can focus on even though it may hurt now, but "weeping only endures for a night and joy will comes in the morning."

Isaiah 26:3 says, "He will have perfect peace who keeps his mind stayed on Him." Focusing on God our Father can take away the hurt of not having an earthly father.

A really good comfort for me is found in Psalm 91. It tells us:

[1] He who dwells in the secret place of the Most High shall abide under the shadow of the Almighty.

[2] I will say of the Lord, "He is my refuge and my fortress; My God, in Him I will trust."

[3] Surely He shall deliver you from the snare of the fowler and from the perilous pestilence.

[4] He shall cover you with His feathers,

And under His wings you shall take refuge; His truth shall be your shield and buckler.

⁵ You shall not be afraid of the terror by night, Nor of the arrow that flies by day,

⁶ Nor of the pestilence that walks in darkness, Nor of the destruction that lays waste at noonday.

⁷ A thousand may fall at your side, And ten thousand at your right hand; But it shall not come near you.

⁸ Only with your eyes shall you look, And see the reward of the wicked.

⁹ Because you have made the Lord, who is my refuge, Even the Most High, your dwelling place,

¹⁰ No evil shall befall you, Nor shall any plague come near your dwelling;

¹¹For He shall give His angels charge over you, To keep you in all your ways.

¹² In their hands they shall bear you up, Lest you dash your foot against a stone.

¹³ You shall tread upon the lion and the cobra, The young lion and the serpent you shall trample underfoot.

¹⁴ Because he has set his love upon Me, therefore I will deliver him; I will set him on high, because he has known My name.

¹⁵ He shall call upon Me, and I will answer him; I will be with him in trouble; I will deliver him and honor him.

¹⁶ With long life I will satisfy him, And show him My salvation."

What a beautiful comfort knowing God loves us so much that He will cover you from it all. A lot of times it is easy to believe we aren't covered when things keep coming our way. However, if you were not covered what would it look like? I have been through some things that weren't my favorite, but I know God was right there with me.

If you are still struggling with uninvited actors and scenes that have written themselves into your life's script, here are some scriptures that will help bring solace and peace to your soul. I recommend that you read them every day and God will show up in your situation and turn it around.

Psalm 55:22

Matthew 11:28-30

Psalm 23

Psalm 118

Psalm 46:10

Psalm 34:17

Philippians 4:6-7

John 16:33

John 14:27

Proverbs 16:7

Now, it's your time...go ahead and rewrite the scene!

Coming soon to a theatre near you

"The Other Woman"

FROM PIECES TO PEACE

Made in the USA
San Bernardino, CA
17 June 2016